Avebury
Monuments and landscape

WILTSHIRE

A souvenir guide

THE NATIONAL TRUST

AVEBURY

Avebury lies at the centre of one of the greatest surviving concentrations of Neolithic and Bronze Age monuments in Western Europe. It is a landscape of excess in terms of monuments: longer, higher, larger, more numerous.

Right Avebury henge and village from the north-east, with the great mound of Silbury Hill beyond. The Avebury bank and ditch, with its internal stone settings, form a 'henge'. The word 'henge' was derived by archaeologists from the name 'Stonehenge' in the 1930s, when a name was needed to apply to a type of site only then being recognised. 'Stonehenge' comes from the Old English word *Stanhengist*, which means 'hanging stones'. This refers to the fact that Anglo-Saxon gallows were composed of two posts and a cross-piece, rather than the more familiar inverted 'L' of historic times: just like, in fact, the great standing stones at Stonehenge

The circle of ditch and bank at Avebury, cut from the underlying chalk rock, encloses the remains of the largest stone circle in the British Isles. The largest prehistoric mound in Europe, Silbury Hill, stands less than a mile to the south, overlooked by one of the longest burial mounds in Britain: West Kennet long barrow. One of the largest settlement sites of the earlier Neolithic period (Windmill Hill) is only a mile to the north, and the remains of the longest avenue of standing stones in the British Isles (West Kennet Avenue) snakes its way south from Avebury towards Overton Hill, a companion to the recently rediscovered Beckhampton Avenue.

Hidden and visible

On both Overton Hill and in the valley of the river Kennet are hidden monuments: the Sanctuary and West Kennet palisaded enclosures were both important elements of the complex in their day, but are now known only from archaeological research. Finally, the most recent monuments of this period, but even so nearly 4,000 years old, all around the landscape and standing as sentinels on the approach from the east, are round burial mounds, raised over the dead of the Early Bronze Age. But not only does the Avebury landscape surprise us with the scale of its obvious monuments. Its history during the last two thousand years, although on a more domestic scale, is also complex and fascinating.

Avebury since Roman times

In the early years of Roman Britain, the main road from London to Bath was aligned using Silbury Hill, and a settlement grew up around its foot, which may have had a religious site associated with it. Four hundred or so years

6,000 years in a day

If you choose a day when the manor house and museum are open, you could in one day's visit go from the earliest dated monuments in the Avebury landscape (Windmill Hill and West Kennet long barrow), to visit the henge and stone circles (passing on the A4 through the site of the Romano-British settlement and parking your car close to the Anglo-Saxon settlement in the main visitor car-park). A walk through the churchyard takes you past the church with Anglo-Saxon features (usually open) and brings you to the manor entrance. Tours of the manor are available on some days, and the gardens are open more frequently). The two galleries of the nearby Alexander Keiller Museum display objects from the excavations and give an introduction to the monuments and landscape.

later, an Anglo-Saxon farmstead or small village stood where visitors now park their cars, and by AD 1000 a large village with a church had developed west of the henge. In the medieval period the village expanded in all directions, and a small priory was founded north-west of the church on a site later occupied by Avebury Manor. By the 18th century Avebury was well known for its monuments, and in the 20th century large excavations were directed at finding out how, when and why the monuments were built.

BEGINNINGS

WINDMILL HILL AND EARLIER NEOLITHIC AVEBURY (4,000–3,000 BC)

If you were suddenly transported back in time to the Avebury area of five and a half thousand years ago, you would expect it to look very different to the way it is today. But as well as the absence of roads, modern buildings and large arable fields, you would notice something else – perhaps something you would not have expected.

4

As well as many more trees than there are now, at 3,500 BC there was no Avebury henge: its great circle of bank and ditch lay nearly a thousand years in the future. There were no circles or avenues of standing stones: they were even more distant in time, probably 1200 to 1400 years ahead; and the huge upturned pudding basin of Silbury Hill, such a dominant feature of a rather unremarkable valley, would also be missing. Not for another millennium would that low-lying site see people gathering to begin the laborious process of putting turf onto turf and chalk block onto chalk block to create the nearly 40m high mound that we see today.

To the north-west of modern Avebury village, however, there is one site which was there in 3,500 BC, a site which was important to Neolithic Avebury and which has played a large part in the recent history of the area. First recorded in the 18th century and first excavated by a local clergyman, Rev. H.G.O. Kendall, in 1922 and 1923, it was interest in Windmill Hill which first brought to the area the man who transformed 20th-century Avebury by re-erecting many of the stones: Alexander Keiller.

Right The view east from Windmill Hill

Below Excavating Windmill Hill in 1926

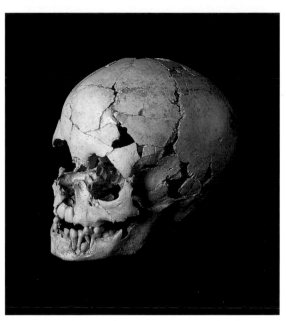

Left Skull of a child of about seven years, found in the middle circuit of the three ditches

Far left Alexander Keiller

Alexander Keiller

From 1925 to 1929 Alexander Keiller, his wife Veronica and sister-in-law Dorothy Liddell, with a team of men from the local area, excavated a large part of a five and a half thousand year old settlement. It was the first large-scale excavation of this type of site and it led to the early Neolithic period of southern Britain being known as the Windmill Hill Culture for most of the 20th century.

Windmill Hill barely looks like a hill from the south, but has a steeper northern slope, and the three concentric rings of ditches which enclose the top of the hill are slightly 'tipped' in that direction, which is also where one of the possible entrances lies. These ditches were first dug between 3,700 and 3,500 BC, and surround an area of about eight hectares (21 acres). In them Alexander Keiller and his team found remains of around 1,300 clay pots, about 95,000 worked flints (flint tools and the waste from making them), thousands of animal bones and smaller quantities of worked chalk and other worked stone.

Traces of the dead

Excavations in 1957, 1958 and 1988 added more information to what is known about Windmill Hill, and it is now clear that it was a site occupied for at least part of every year – at least spring to autumn – for about three hundred years. Later on, the hill seems to have been used occasionally for several centuries more. As well as all the activities which have left traces, there must also have been many which left none. Animals would have been traded and exchanged, and people would have passed through stages of life and death that would probably have been marked by ceremonies. Some of the people who lived at Windmill Hill are still there, or at least parts of them are. In the three campaigns of excavation in the 20th century there were around 40 finds of human remains, and others may lie in the unexcavated parts of the site. Most people were represented only by single bones or a small number of bones or teeth, and there were only three complete burials (a man, a child and a baby). Many of the remains were of children. Almost more than anything else, this treatment of the dead brings home to us the difference between our own time and this distant past.

There is a 40–50 minute walk from Avebury village along footpaths. Maps and guides are available from the Alexander Keiller Museum.

WEST KENNET LONG BARROW (From 3,700 BC)

The people of early Neolithic Avebury may not have gone as far in large scale construction projects as their successors did a thousand years later, but they certainly left their mark on the landscape. In a few hundred years in the earlier part of the Neolithic period the people of the Avebury area constructed around fourteen long burial mounds within a radius of three miles from Avebury village. There are even more, if the Avebury area is considered to extend towards Marlborough, Devizes and Calne.

West Kennet long barrow is open every day (no charge). Cars may be parked in two lay-bys on the A4 west of West Kennett village. The site is reached by a 700m walk uphill.

These burial mounds vary from 20m to just over 100m in length, although most are in the range 30–60m. The longest, and one of the longest in the British Isles, is West Kennet long barrow, 1.2 miles due south of Avebury.

These were not small projects, but involved digging large, deep ditches through chalk and, in several cases, moving stones weighing several tonnes, setting them upright, and balancing them flat on the upright stones to form roofed chambers. West Kennet is one of the barrows that certainly contains burial chambers, and it is the only one in the Avebury area in which the chambers can be visited today.

West Kennet long barrow has been excavated on two occasions, in 1859 and in 1955–6. These excavations revealed five chambers within the barrow, linked by a corridor, all in the eastern 12m of the mound.

Human remains were found in all five chambers; most of these date from the first use of the mound for burial, but some have proved to be several hundred years later in date. During the main, early, period of use, there is some evidence that people were placed in the chambers according to a pattern: in the end (western) chamber there were only adult males and one child (sex not identified); in the back left (south-western) chamber adults and adolescents; in the back right (north-western) seven adults and one child; in the right front (north-eastern) only adults, and in the front left (south-eastern) more children (five) than adults (two). It was in this chamber too that most of the later burials were placed, all of young children and babies.

A programme of radiocarbon dating by Cardiff University and English Heritage has shown that the mound was built and most of the burials placed in it during a very short initial period, probably in the middle decades of the 37th century BC (3,700–3,600 BC). Following this, the chambers were probably filled in over several hundred years with chalk rubble and debris including pottery, animal bone, beads of bone, stone and shell and worked flint tools. Within and on top of this were the later human remains, mainly of children, which date from about 3,300 BC to possibly as late as 2,500 BC.

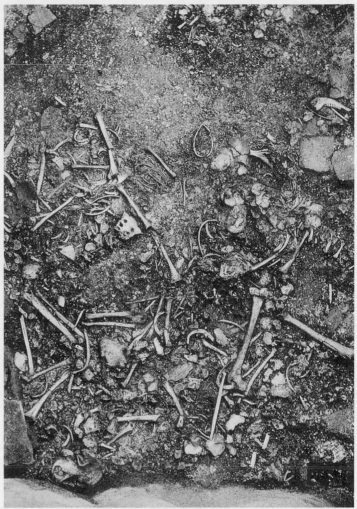

Remains of about 36 people were placed in the West Kennet long barrow chambers soon after it was first built. Many of the people represented by human remains from West Kennet are not complete skeletons. In some long barrows this may be the result of secondary burial, in which bodies are allowed to decay and become bone elsewhere before being placed in the chambers. At West Kennet, however, it seems that the dead were placed in the chambers as complete bodies, and the bones later moved around and reorganized. Some bones seem to have been removed altogether, perhaps for ceremonies or burial elsewhere.

Above left West Kennet long barrow **Left** The interior of the tomb

THE HENGE – BANK AND DITCH (2,600 BC)

The scale of Avebury is a surprise: just over three-quarters of a mile around its bank, about 340m across the interior, the visible ditch 20m across and 3–4m deep enclosing around 11 hectares (28 acres). It is impressive now, but its physical presence today is a blunted and mellowed version of what it would have been when newly built.

In a landscape which we know was, by four and a half thousand years ago, largely grass downland, the white chalk wall of the bank cutting off the interior from the outside world must have seemed a startling departure from the normal, natural order of things. A construction project this size would still be impressive if it were undertaken today; as the product of a society which had no earth-moving devices except people's own hands, it seems astonishing. On present dating evidence, it seems that this work of levering out the solid chalk to a depth of, originally, more than 9m and forming it into a bank over 4m high was undertaken probably around 2,600 BC, at least a couple of centuries before most of the stones were erected. Even without having to move stones at the same time, the work entailed was enormous: it has been calculated that about 1.5 million work hours went into it, and these

Left The ditch near the southern entrance, under excavation in 1914. It was originally just over 9m deep from the present ground surface inside the henge. It was originally narrower too, the gentle v-shape of the upper ditch being the result of weathering of the sides. When first dug, the ditch would have been dizzying to look down into, its sides falling sharply to the base many metres below

were hours of work with antler picks and rakes, breaking up chalk and raking it into baskets to be hauled up ladders or handled by chains of labourers to add to the bank.

Why was Avebury built?

This question is almost impossible to answer, but if other societies that have undertaken great works are considered, some reasons emerge: it may have been a place for celebrating important times in the year; or for marking important – often transitional – times in people's lives, or their departure from life; or for making contact with ancestors, or with supernatural beings or forces, often with the hope or intention of influencing matters in their own lives. If Avebury was a special or sacred place, it might also have been considered a dangerous one, where powerful forces were to be kept in, or out. The great work of the bank or ditch, so impressive, but inexplicable to us, would have seemed eminently practical and necessary to its makers.

Why here?

Perhaps because there was already something on the site which made it important. In two locations around the bank, in the south-eastern sector, and in the south-western, small excavations have revealed a feature which seems to be an earlier bank, buried deep within the present one.

If this is the case, then there may already have been a smaller version of Avebury here a few years, or a few centuries, earlier than the bank and ditch we see today. Unfortunately, there is no evidence as to what such an early enclosure was for or exactly what form it took, but it may be close in date to the bank and ditch at Stonehenge. There a bank and ditch were created around a circular area 100m across, 400 or so years before the first stones were erected in the circles. This may have been part of a change, at around 3,000–2,900 BC, in how people viewed the world in this part of Britain.

Below The ditch in the south-west sector

STONES

Avebury henge stands within a landscape of stone, more obvious in the Neolithic period than today. Wiltshire is chalk country, with rounded outlines to its hills reflecting the soft rock beneath the turf which originated in the seas of 100 million years ago. But the northern Downs, especially around Avebury and Marlborough, are spectacularly littered with a younger rock, one of the hardest, most intractable rocks of the British Isles: sarsen. This is a hard, grey sandstone, with quartz grains glittering in a silica matrix. Some of it is called 'saccharoidal' – sugar-like – and when freshly broken looks very like hard-packed grains of sugar.

Right Piggledene, east of Avebury. This gives an impression of what much of the countryside around Avebury would have looked like, particularly to the east, in the past. Some of the stones also show traces of the 19th-century sarsen-working industry that once flourished here

Sarsen formed about 30–35 million years ago, above the chalk, and probably just below the then ground surface. Changes to the ground water seem to have caused silica to form a cement, binding together grains of sand. Sarsens now lie in 'trains' along the bottom of valleys in the downs. Alternative theories explain this: either by suggesting that the sarsen was broken up and slumped down slopes during Ice Age cycles of freeze and thaw, or that the sarsens formed in the valleys. Holes in the stones are the result of the decay of roots growing down into the sand from plants including palms, and many of these can be seen on the Avebury stones.

What's in a name?

'Sarsen' may be derived from 'Saracen', in the past used to mean something or someone foreign, or, alternatively, it may come from the Old English *sar stan* meaning 'troublesome stone', because they often lie just below the surface, where they are a nuisance when ploughing. Another local name for the stones lying naturally in fields is 'grey wethers', wethers being sheep, which they resemble at a distance.

Why stone?

There is no way of knowing how the standing stones at Avebury were regarded when they were first put up, but the choice of stone was obviously a deliberate one. Some people suggest that stone may have been used in places where ancestors were important, while timber was more usual in places used by the living. Even today, stone is used to commemorate the dead, because of its resistance to decay.

Above Excavation around the base of the Swindon Stone in 1937 demonstrated that it is not set very deep in the ground, and this was true of most of the stones

Left Known today as the Swindon Stone or Diamond Stone, this large stone flanks the northern entrance to the henge. Until the 18th century it seems to have had a tall, straighter partner on the other side of the entrance. This pairing of straight and diamond stones may reflect male and female aspects, and also occurs on the West Kennet Avenue. The shape is natural and, unlike many stones at Avebury, this stone has not been moved since the Neolithic period. It is estimated to weigh about 60 tonnes

CIRCLES WITHIN CIRCLES

Above Reconstruction of the henge as it may have been when new, showing the positions of all the stones

Within the encircling bank and ditch, the great Outer Circle of Avebury once held around 100 standing stones and was the largest stone circle in the British Isles. Arranged north and south inside it, stood two inner circles of large stones, with probably around 30 stones in each. Within those in turn stood more stones: in the Southern Circle there were a rectangular or trapezoid setting of small (chest-high) stones, of which a line now remains, and a tall pillar of sarsen (known as the Obelisk), which was broken up in the 18th century and is now marked by a large pyramid-shaped concrete marker; in the Northern Circle a now-buried setting of stones, possibly in curving rows, and at its centre three huge stones, two of which still stand (known as the Cove).

The Ring Stone

Only one stone lies completely outside these circles, and that was a special stone in its own right: the Ring Stone. Seen as a small standing stone in the 18th century, it appears to have had a perforation close to its top. There is no clear reason for its location, but it would have been a very obvious feature to anyone entering the henge from the southern entrance. One other stone, its position now marked by a concrete marker, stood close to where a large stone now flanks the northern entrance and cannot have stood at the same time as the entrance stone. This is a hint that there was a history of change to the stone settings, but not one we are at present able to understand.

Returning the stones

Of all these standing stones within the henge, only fifteen survived upright until the 20th century, and 36 are now standing. During excavations in the 1930s Alexander Keiller found the extra 21 buried or fallen and put them back up, either in the holes which had previously held them or as near as he could estimate to their former positions.

Celebrating cycles

It seems obvious that these circles and settings must have held special meanings for the users of Avebury in the Neolithic period, but they have left us very few clues as to what they were doing or what Avebury meant to them. All we have are the few objects left by the users and the way the site is laid out – and then we have to use our imaginations.

Many people think that stone circles were connected with observing the sky and holding celebrations associated with the cycle of the

Above Stones in the south-east sector

year, or the cycles over several years of the moon or sun. Many societies have done this, but at Avebury the site is so large and so damaged that it is difficult to identify evidence for alignments on particular celestial bodies which is at all convincing. More tangibly, it is interesting to consider how the site may have been used in a physical way. Some people have suggested that the banks were used for viewing events happening in the interior, but others argue that the bank and ditch and the imposing lines of stone were meant to exclude people. Even today, in many religious buildings there are areas set aside for priests and their assistants that the wider congregation is kept out of. In some cases, in some cultures, areas are set aside for the dead or for the supernatural; it may be that no ordinary person was meant to venture inside the pale excluding wall of the henge. Perhaps only the dead were expected to walk there, isolated on their artificial island, separated from the world of the living by the 9m deep ditch and tended by a very few.

AVENUES

Below The pairing of diamond-shaped stone and straight stone occurs elsewhere on the West Kennet Avenue, and probably also once did in the henge at the northern entrance. The shapes may represent femaleness and maleness

No-one saw Avebury from the air when all the stones were standing, but if they had been able to, they would also have seen two double sinuous trails of standing stones snaking away across the landscape to south-east and south-west from the entrances to the henge. These two features are now known as the West Kennet and Beckhampton Avenues. It is possible, although there is no proof yet, that there were once four avenues, one extending from each entrance.

The West Kennet Avenue

The West Kennet Avenue is the better known of the two and can be followed easily for the northern third of its length. When new, there were probably around 100 pairs of standing stones, each pair arranged roughly 20–30m from the next pair with the stones of each pair standing around 15m apart. The Avenue ran for about 1.6 miles from the southern entrance of Avebury henge to a double stone circle on Overton Hill, now known as the Sanctuary (see p.20).

The Beckhampton Avenue

To the west, leaving Avebury henge by what is now the High Street, was a similar avenue of paired stones leading in the direction of the present hamlet of Beckhampton. Only a few stones visibly survived of this, even in the 18th century, and for many years its existence was doubted. But in 1999 stones from this avenue were rediscovered as part of a project run by three universities to test for its existence. Four stones were found buried, and the places where five more had once stood were identified from the traces of stone destruction left by people who had broken up the stones. The same project found the end of the Beckhampton Avenue, where it was at first closed with a blocking arrangement of three stones, later replaced by a setting of four stones in an open 'box' shape. The remains of this were known in the 18th century and were termed a 'cove', similar to a setting of the same name within Avebury henge (see p.16).

The Longstones

At the far end of the Beckhampton Avenue two stones are still standing, known as the Longstones. One of these, 'Adam', was part of the Cove, while the other, 'Eve', formed part of the avenue itself. At this end too there was an earlier enclosure, an oval area surrounded by a ditch and bank. This seems to have been made not long before the large ditch at Avebury henge was dug. In this case the enclosure must have gone out of use when the avenue was built, or slightly earlier, and the ditch was filled in deliberately.

Above and **left** The West Kennet Avenue

THE COVE

Close to the road in the north-east quadrant of the henge are two of the tallest stones at Avebury. These form part of what has been known as the Cove since the 18th century, named by the antiquary William Stukeley. Until 1713 (according to Stukeley) this setting had a third stone, standing as a pair to the tall, slim southern stone and forming, with the other two, a space rather like a stage without a roof. More than anywhere else within the henge the Cove seems a place which hints at past activities, perhaps performances and ceremonies.

Right The Cove photographed in the mid-1860s, looking west. The houses standing close to it were demolished in the late 1950s

Observing the heavens

Standing within the Cove and looking outwards, the view is eastwards, towards the high ground of the Marlborough Downs and to the eastern sky. The orientation can only be approximate, as the structure is several metres broad, but it is towards the north-east. It has been suggested that it may have been directed towards observing moon rise at a major point in the moon's 18.6-year cycle, but this cannot be certain. The sun (which rises in the north-east at midsummer) also seems to have been important in the later Neolithic period, as the significance of its summer solstice rising or winter solstice setting demonstrates at Stonehenge, but there are many societies in which not only the sun, but also the moon, stars and planets are observed. Stars are visible markers for the seasons, as for instance the appearance of the constellation known as the Swan heralding the summer, or the disappearance of Orion from the night sky reminding us that the long cold months are nearly over, but the possibilities are so many that hope of identifying site-specific ones for Avebury is slim, and none is convincing. However, it does seems likely that the users of Avebury stood in the Cove to observe the movements of celestial bodies in the day and night sky above their heads.

Of the Cove as a structure, little is known. Only very small-scale excavation has taken place in modern times, although in the 19th century there were at least two episodes of digging. In 2003 excavations beside both stones showed that the large 'back stone' was by a long way the largest stone now on site. Some writers have pointed out the resemblance between the chambers of long barrows like the local West Kennet long barrow and the box-

like structure of the Cove and the few other 'coves' known. The long barrow chambers are many centuries earlier in date, but the resemblance with West Kennet is particularly striking. There is no reason to believe that the Cove was a funerary monument, but the resemblance may be a deliberate harking back to a structure recognized as connected with the past and with the long dead.

Above The Cove from the west; the stone facing the camera has an overall length of about 7m, and weighs about 100 tonnes. This makes it by far the heaviest standing stone in the British Isles. A relatively new technique of dating, called optically stimulated luminescence, has produced a date of 3030 +/- 350 BC for the erection of the stone. This gives a large range, but it may be that, given its size, this stone was not brought far, and may have been the first feature at Avebury

Above left The Cove

SILBURY HILL (2,400–2,000 BC)

The later part of the third millennium BC, particularly from about 2,600 BC onwards, was a time of great enterprises. People were motivated to take on tasks which, given the resources they had at the time, seem barely achievable. But they did achieve them: the henge with its great circles of stone at Avebury and other great henges elsewhere; building in stone in a unique way at Stonehenge; and, in the valley of the Kennet, by building Silbury Hill, the largest prehistoric mound in Europe, around 37m high, 30m across its top and about 500m around its base.

Opposite Silbury Hill is the largest prehistoric mound in Europe

Above Silbury Hill occupies a valley-floor position, close to where the River Kennet rises at Swallowhead Springs and where it is joined from the north by the Winterbourne stream, which, as its name suggests, runs mostly in the winter. Silbury Hill is privately owned and is managed by English Heritage. There is no public access to the hill

Like journeys which begin with a single step, Silbury began with a single load of soil and gravel – or, at least, with no more than a few basketfuls. These were followed by soil and by turf cut from surrounding meadows, and probably also from areas of grass further away. A lot is known about this material, as excavations in 1968–9 produced preserved pollen, mosses, plant fragments, seeds, grasses and abundant insect remains, including beetles and ants. Work by English Heritage in 2007, primarily to stabilize the hill, has produced much more evidence which has been undergoing analysis.

Radiocarbon dating has offered some evidence as to when the hill was built. There are two possible interpretations of the dates, neither of which can yet be proved beyond doubt. The builders seem to have begun the hill at around 2400 BC, but it is not clear when the work was finished. One interpretation of the present evidence is that it reached its final form fairly quickly, in about 100 years, but an alternative interpretation is that it was not finished until about 2,000 BC, (i.e. 350–400 years after it was started).

The excavations of 1968–9 largely followed the line of a tunnel dug into the hill in 1849. Neither episode of tunnelling found anything at the centre to explain why the hill was built, but did establish how it was made. After the first very small mound of gravel and clay there was a larger mound mainly of turf and soil surviving in its compressed form to over 2m high. This mound was covered with a capping of chalk and soil to a height of just over 5m, and only after that was the main mound built, probably in at least two stages. The first of these used chalk from a ditch or quarries now buried under the mound, while the last, outer, stage of the mound used chalk dug from a huge ditch and ditch extension.

The 2007 work identified even more late Neolithic phases of construction, suggesting that the mound grew through many small events rather than a few grand statements.

THE SANCTUARY (2,500–2,000 BC)

Wood into stone

Today the site known as the Sanctuary is easy to miss. Cars speed past it as they travel along the A4 from Marlborough or Calne. Coming from the east the eye is caught more readily by the impressive Bronze Age round barrows to the north of the road than by the small fenced area to the south which surrounds an array of concrete markers. But 4,000 years ago this site was a double stone circle, linked to Avebury henge, just over 1.2 miles to the north-west, not just by ties of common use, but also by a more tangible link of stone: 100 or so pairs of standing stones which formed the West Kennet Avenue.

Circles of timber

The Sanctuary probably began as a setting of timber posts arranged in concentric circles, with a maximum diameter of about 20m. Some of the timbers may have had lintels joining them at the top, like the sarsen circle and trilithons at Stonehenge, where techniques used on the stones were clearly derived from wood-working. Pottery, including 'Grooved Ware',

which is often found at henges, was found deep in some of the postholes at the Sanctuary. Although there are no radiocarbon dates for this timber structure, it can probably be dated to the centuries around 2,500 BC on the grounds of the artefacts found in the postholes.

It seems that, while at least some of the posts were still standing, a double stone circle was put up, using sarsen stones, which was twice the diameter of the timber circles. This must have happened before the West Kennet Avenue was built, or while it was being built, as the Avenue narrows to join the stone circle, and there is no evidence that it had ever joined the timber circles. It is not certain when the stone circle was built, but it may have continued in use until around 2000 BC. The burial of a young man with a Beaker pot, next to one of the stones, probably dates to around this time.

The Sanctuary is open at all times. It is managed by the National Trust under an agreement with English Heritage on behalf of the nation.

Above The location of the Sanctuary was rediscovered by two Wiltshire archaeologists, Benjamin and Maud Cunnington, who excavated the site in 1930. The picture shows men standing in some of the holes which had held posts. Benjamin Cunnington is standing between them

Left William Stukeley, who recorded the Avebury monuments in the 18th century, also visited the Sanctuary. This view shows how he saw it in July 1723. He commented that he 'happen'd to frequent this place in the very point in time, when there was a possibility just left, of preserving the memory of it'. He records the names of two farmers who were involved in its destruction and records that the stones were taken to Beckhampton for building by Farmer Green and that Farmer Griffin ploughed up half the site

DEATH AND BURIAL IN THE BRONZE AGE

All around Avebury are reminders of the Bronze Age dead. Four thousand years ago there were at least a hundred round burial mounds, most showing clean white chalk, on many of the higher places on the downs immediately around Avebury, and some of them on lower ground. Each of these was raised over the burial of a man, woman or child, and many covered more than one individual. Many of these mounds, now known as 'barrows', would have originally stood as tall as a person and measured several metres across. Nowadays many are no longer visible, ploughed flat after centuries of farming, but some survive: here are some which you can visit, or which can be seen from publicly accessible land.

Overton Hill

Just to the north of the A4 (left as you go towards Marlborough). This barrow cemetery, also crossed by the much more recent Roman road from London to Bath, is one of the best preserved in the country. Only one of the Bronze Age barrows has been excavated in recent times, revealing evidence of twelve people (six inhumations and six cremations), only five of whom were adults, the others being children (three) or babies (four). The first burial, probably without a mound, was of a man, possibly buried in a fur cape, with a Beaker pot and objects of stone, antler and metal which may be a leatherworker's set of tools.

Right Barrows were often sited to be seen as prominent features on the horizon, and in the 18th and 19th centuries groups of trees were often planted on them (known locally as 'hedgehogs')

*The barrow field is NT land and open to the public; there is parking on the Ridgeway (not NT). It is **not** recommended that you cross the A4 to or from the Sanctuary here.*

Windmill Hill

A large barrow cemetery once stood here, extending down the hill towards Avebury, but few of the barrows have survived. Of those that do survive, there are several good examples, of which one of the best is known as Picket Barrow.

Windmill Hill is best reached on foot; there is a pleasant walk along public footpaths from Avebury.

East and south of Avebury

From the southern bank of the henge there is a good view of barrows on the horizon to the east. Also visible from the henge, on Waden Hill, overlooking the West Kennet Avenue, there was once a large barrow cemetery, now long since ploughed flat.

BURYING STONES

One of the most mysterious features of the monuments is nothing at all to do with what happened in prehistory. It is the fact that for a time in the Middle Ages, and perhaps until the 16th century, local people invested time and expense in the dangerous practice of pulling down standing stones and burying them underground.

In the 18th century William Stukeley recorded that stones had been buried in 'great pits in the earth'. In the 19th century two clergymen – A.C. Smith and W.C. Lukis – demonstrated by probing that there were many buried stones lying under the turf. In the 1930s ten buried stones of the Outer Circle were found and re-erected by Alexander Keiller, and others have been located precisely by geophysical surveys.

The 'Barber Surgeon'

It was also Alexander Keiller who first found evidence for the date of some of the stone burials. On 29 June 1938 he described in a letter making an unexpected find alongside one of the buried stones: 'a skeleton found pressed up against one side of the burial pit of stone 38 [now 9] ... this skeleton turned out (to cut a long story as short as I can) to be that of an

Below The Barber Surgeon stone

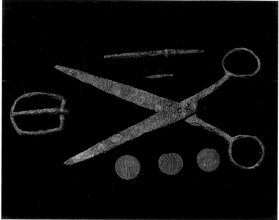

Above These coins found with the 'barber surgeon' suggest that he died in the early part of the 14th century, possibly in the 1320s. The close dating of the coins also makes the scissors found with them one of the earliest pairs of true scissors in the British Isles

individual killed by the falling, or slipping of the stone during the process of burial.'

The skeleton was of a man, with a healed cut to the head, possibly caused by a sword. He appeared to have been pinned to the side of the hole by the stone and may have died of internal injuries. At first Alexander Keiller thought he might have been a tailor because a pair of scissors and a metal point were found with him, but later changed this to a barber surgeon. (His own ancestors had been 'chirugeon barbers' on Scottish whalers). In truth, either could be correct, or neither.

It has been suggested that this man was not killed by the stone falling and pinning him to the side of the pit but that he had died in some other way and been put into the pit dead, but this is uncertain. Even if this particular event were not an accident it does not take much imagination to see that felling and burying stones must have been dangerous and there must have been some compelling reason for it. So what was it?

Why bury stones?

Two possible reasons are usually mentioned for burying stones. One is that the stones were in the way of agricultural practices and were buried rather than broken up because the method of breaking the hard stone was not fully understood or practised. The other frequently mentioned reason for burial is that the church could have encouraged or ordered the local people to bury stones because they were associated with pagan practices or were in some way thought to be non-Christian. Unfortunately, there is no 14th-century documentary evidence to support or refute either argument, and the mystery remains.

Above The 'barber surgeon' as found

DESTRUCTION

At the time of the Battle of Hastings (AD 1066) it is likely that most of the standing stones in the stone circles and avenues at Avebury, West Kennet and Beckhampton were still standing. By 1908, when the first large-scale excavations began, only fifteen were left upright in the henge, two at Beckhampton, and four in the West Kennet Avenue. What was it, then, that had happened to them in the 842 years in between to bring that about?

Trial by fire

Not all the missing stones had disappeared from the site in that time. Many of the stones had been buried in the Middle Ages or shortly afterwards, but many had been broken up, and some had been used for building locally. William Stukeley, visiting Avebury in the early 18th century, recorded the local story that the method of breaking the stones up by heating them had been invented by a local man in the late 17th century, but archaeological evidence shows that this cannot be correct. For instance, although the beginning of this practice is not documented, there are pieces of broken sarsen in 15th-century work in the church and at the site of Falkner's Circle – a probable small stone circle 800m south of the henge – a radio-carbon date for a destroyed stone shows that breaking stones using fire may have been taking place as early as the 16th century or even the late 15th century.

Right Tom Robinson was called 'the Herostratus of Avebury' by Stukeley, which is a classical allusion to the destroyer of the Temple of Artemis at Ephesus. But his facts were not always correct, probably because Stukeley was sometimes reporting events which had happened several years before his own visits. Stukeley's plans are marked with the dates at which stones were destroyed and by whom, but some of those marked as destroyed by Tom Robinson we now know are still there beneath the turf in the south-eastern part of the site

Opposite The process of stone-breaking usually consisted of digging a pit close to the stone, filling it with straw and felling the stone onto it. The stone was heated by firing the pit and then doused with cold water, causing cracks to appear

The *main* period of destruction of stones, however, *is* well documented, as William Stukeley, who had been alerted to Avebury's monuments probably through the work of the 17th-century antiquary John Aubrey, made several visits to Avebury in the early 18th century at a time when much of the destruction was occurring. He recorded the henge and surrounding sites between 1719 and 1724 and wrote descriptions of the stone-breaking, and of the stone breakers. Stukeley named six local farmers as being particularly responsible, one of whom, Tom Robinson, he illustrated in his book *Abury*, published in 1743.

Sarsens were used in many of the village buildings and in stone walls, a rare advantage in a county largely having only soft rock for building (ie chalk). Sarsens from the surrounding countryside were also taken until very recent times, particularly for setts (pavement stones – there are some in Avebury High Street and near the museum). More unusual uses include sarsens taken in the early 19th century from nearby Lockeridge by the then Duke of Marlborough to be used in a garden folly at Whiteknights` House, now part of the University of Reading. Alexander Keiller notes a search in the 1930s for one to form a memorial stone for the poet Edward Thomas.

AVEBURY PEOPLE

John Aubrey (1626–97)
The monuments at Avebury existed in rural obscurity until the 17th century, objects of curiosity to local people perhaps, or accepted as natural features of the landscape. Then, in the winter of 1649, a young Wiltshire gentleman, John Aubrey of Kington St Michael, was hunting with some friends from Marlborough Castle when he stumbled across the Avebury standing stones and realised that here was something rather extraordinary. Even so, it was not until 1663, when Aubrey was moving in exalted London circles, that he helped to make Avebury famous. From then onwards, for more than 300 years, people have studied Avebury and sought to understand its monuments.

Above John Aubrey; by Faithorne

'Rude circles'

'I was wonderfully surprized at the sight of those vast stones, of which I had never heard before .... I observed in the Inclosures some segments of rude circles, made with those stones: whence I concluded, they had been in the old time complete.'

John Aubrey

Above William Stukeley; by Godfrey Kneller

Below Sir Richard Colt Hoare

AVEBURY PEOPLE

William Stukeley (1687–1765)

William Stukeley's career began in medicine and he was later a clergyman but he is best known for his work at Avebury, Stonehenge and other prehistoric monuments in the early 18th century. Anyone interested in Avebury today owes a debt of gratitude to Stukeley for recording many of the monuments at the very time that they were being destroyed to produce building stone.

Between 1719 and 1724 Stukeley made annual visits to Avebury, staying about two weeks on each occasion. He seems usually to have stayed at the Catherine Wheel, an inn which lay within the north-east sector close to the setting known as the Cove. From his measured drawings, sketches and notes he produced his book *Abury*. This, with a large surviving quantity of notes and drawings, many of which are now in the Bodleian Library at Oxford, has left us an invaluable picture of Avebury as it was before much of it was destroyed, and Stukeley's work also contributed to the rediscovery in the 20th century of two important monuments: the Sanctuary and the Beckhampton Avenue (see p.14, 20).

18th- and 19th-century investigations

Following William Stukeley's work in the early 18th century there was a major investigation of Silbury Hill when a shaft was dug from top to bottom by the Duke of Northumberland in 1776–7. No central burial was found. In the early 19th century the Wiltshire antiquaries William Cunnington and Sir Richard Colt Hoare explored a number of Bronze Age burial mounds in the local area, but the next major excavation was at Silbury Hill.

In 1849 a long tunnel was dug into the heart of Silbury Hill, mainly to establish whether there was a central burial. The Dean of Hereford Cathedral, John Merewether, who directed the excavation on behalf of the Archaeological Institute, also took the opportunity of being in the Avebury area to dig into more than 30 round barrows in three weeks.

20th-century excavators: Harold St George Gray and Alexander Keiller

Between 1908 and 1922 Harold St George Gray, an experienced archaeologist employed by the British Association, dug for five excavation seasons at Avebury. He cut five trenches into the ditch, all in the southern part of the site, and one into the bank. He proved that the ditch was originally very much deeper than it appears now, more than 9m deep below the present interior of the henge, for instance, beside the southern entrance. Gray also found many antler picks, which were used to build the ditch and bank, and smaller numbers of other finds, including small amounts of human bone and one complete burial of a small adult woman beside the southern entrance.

Twelve years after Gray's last season of digging, Alexander Keiller, of a family who manufactured a well-known make of marmalade, began excavations on the West Kennet Avenue. He had already dug for parts of five summers on the Neolithic site at Windmill Hill, just over a mile north-west of Avebury, and by the time he finished excavating at Avebury, in 1939, he had dug for a further five summers on the West Kennet Avenue and henge.

Alexander Keiller's work at Avebury included the excavation of a third of the West Kennet Avenue and about half the Outer Circle of stones in the henge with some of the interior, but he also reconstructed some of the stone settings. In the Middle Ages and perhaps later many of the stones had been buried and where Alexander Keiller found these, he re-erected them as close to their original positions as possible, as he also did with fallen stones; where stones had been destroyed, he marked their position with concrete posts which he designed himself. Although he did not finish all the work he had planned, his re-erection of 50 stones in the henge and West Kennet Avenue made a striking difference to the appearance of the site. In 1938 he opened an on-site museum, now known as the Alexander Keiller Museum, which houses the records and artefacts from his excavations and from later work around Avebury. More controversially, he also demolished some village buildings, and more were removed in the 1950s by the National Trust. This was with the intention of returning the site to its prehistoric condition, but was abandoned in the 1960s.

Below Alexander Keiller

Far left Dean Merewether
Left Harold St George Gray

AVEBURY CHURCH AND VILLAGE

Many English villages can trace their beginnings to Anglo-Saxon times, but very few have any surviving Anglo-Saxon buildings which you can walk into. Avebury is one of those few, as parts of the pre-conquest church, a thousand years old, are still visible within the present church.

Anglo-Saxon Avebury

Avebury's Anglo-Saxon past began a hundred years or so after the end of Roman Britain, when a small village or farmstead was settled where the modern visitor car-park now lies, west of the henge and close to the Winterbourne stream. At least two huts, with sunken floors (or underfloor-pits) were excavated near the road in 1976, and other structures were later found in the northern part of the car-park. This settlement can be dated probably to between AD 500 and AD 600 on the basis of three decorated glass beads. This small village or farm lies just to the north of a very large Romano-British roadside settlement which ran north along the valley of the Winterbourne from Silbury Hill, and south from the hill to the source of the River Kennet at Swallowhead Springs, straddling the Roman road from London to Bath.

In the centuries leading up to AD 1000 a larger village grew up to the north of the earlier settlements; this partly underlies the present village. It was a village of wooden buildings, most standing within ditched enclosures, and the whole village may have been surrounded by a bank and ditch as a 'burgh' (a defended settlement). The villagers living here would have seen the building of the stone church, a few metres outside the bank of the henge (the bank is now no longer visible in the churchyard).

The name 'Avebury' dates from this period, but there is no agreement over what it means, except that the 'bury' part means a defended place. The first part of the name may be from the British for river, or it could be a personal Anglo-Saxon name.

The church was founded around AD 1000 and appears to have been a 'minster' church, that is, a church held by the crown and serving a large area. Like many Anglo-Saxon churches, the building was simple and very tall for its width.

The Church of St James is usually open every day from about 10.00 am to dusk.

Opposite Avebury church
Below A thatched cottage in Avebury village

AVEBURY MANOR

People have lived where Avebury Manor and garden are now for at least 900 years, and probably longer. When excavations took place in the gardens in the 1990s, a complex of ditches and other features showed that there was a complicated history to the site which must pre-date the present manor.

The manor's recorded history began in the early 12th century, when the Abbey of St Georges de Boscherville in Normandy was allowed to set up a small priory at Avebury, where a relatively small number of monks, with hired help, ran a large estate. Six hundred sheep were recorded in a document of 1324/5, and the same source describes the priory as comprising a hall, kitchen, bakehouse, brewhouse, cellar and dairy. The same inventory records a limited number of possessions, including two beds, religious items such as a missal and a breviary, and one luxury – a chess set. The last prior, Stephen Fosse, was expelled in 1378 and took with him a monk, John Santell, and two servants, William Brisey and Thomas Durant. So, after more than 250 years, the connection with Normandy ceased. Subsequently the manor was cared for by royal servants, and from 1411 was in the hands of Fotheringay College in Northamptonshire.

The first written description of the manor dates from 1548, when a steward's report was drawn up for William Sharington, who had been granted it the previous year. The steward describes a building which had both 'old' and 'new' parts. Sharington held the house only for a short time, selling it in 1551 for £2,200. In the 1730s Richard Holford turned the Hall into a dining room and remodelled the Great Chamber above. The house gradually declined during the 19th century until it was taken on in 1902 by Leopold and Nora Jenner, who lovingly restored it and created the present garden. From 1935 it was the home of the archaeologist Alexander Keiller.

Opposite The east front of Avebury Manor. In the 1930s the manor became the home of the archaeologist Alexander Keiller and the location of his 'Morven Institute of Archaeological Research'

Left The south front of Avebury Manor, showing the South Porch, which bears the date '1601' and initials 'M.J.D.'. These are thought to relate to James and Deborah Mervyn, owners in the late 16th and early 17th centuries. The date appears to relate only to the building of the porch

WILD AVEBURY

The chalk landscape around Avebury looks as it does at least in part because of the use made of it by people over six and more millennia. Even so, there is much that is still wild about the landscape, some of it visible even on a short visit, some more hidden. The National Trust regularly monitors its properties and carries out biological surveys so that their biological diversity can be identified, protected and increased.

Bottom right Natterer's bat **Bottom** Barn owl **Below** Polecat

Plants

The banks of the henge have two important plants: the round headed rampion and a hybrid form of the tuberous thistle. Even the stones are an important habitat for lichens. Elsewhere, the Neolithic causewayed enclosure on Windmill Hill occupies a very flowery hilltop, with chalk grassland plants such as dropwort and clustered bellflower. Silbury Hill is a Site of Special Scientific Interest because of its calcareous grassland habitat, unusually facing all the points of the compass within a very small area.

Mammals

Polecats have been found as road casualties close to National Trust property, and brown hares are widespread. The exhibition gallery of the Alexander Keiller Museum in the 17th-century barn is home for part of the year to five species of bats: Natterer's, Pipistrelle, Soprano Pipistrelle, Brown long-eared and Serotine. Observation has shown that many of these feed on insects flying in the ditch of the north-west sector of the henge and among the trees of the manor park.

Birds

There is a colony of tree sparrows on tenanted land close to the henge, and Windmill Hill has grey partridge, yellowhammer, corn bunting and skylark. Barn owls can be seen flying at dusk and are known to roost in some National Trust buildings.